EMMANUEL JOSEPH

The Cross-Continental Moguls, Billionaires Who Bridge Countries and Cultures

Copyright © 2025 by Emmanuel Joseph

All rights reserved. No part of this publication may be reproduced, stored or transmitted in any form or by any means, electronic, mechanical, photocopying, recording, scanning, or otherwise without written permission from the publisher. It is illegal to copy this book, post it to a website, or distribute it by any other means without permission.

First edition

This book was professionally typeset on Reedsy. Find out more at reedsy.com

Contents

1	Chapter 1: The Global Visionaries	1
2	Chapter 2: The Early Days	3
3	Chapter 3: Strategic Alliances	5
4	Chapter 4: Cultural Diplomacy	7
5	Chapter 5: Market Domination	9
6	Chapter 6: The Role of Technology	11
7	Chapter 7: Philanthropy Without Borders	12
8	Chapter 8: Crisis Management	14
9	Chapter 9: Leadership Styles	16
10	Chapter 10: The Power of Branding	18
11	Chapter 11: Mentorship and Legacy	20
12	Chapter 12: Sustainable Ventures	22
13	Chapter 13: Navigating Regulatory Hurdles	24
14	Chapter 14: Innovation and Adaptation	26
15	Chapter 15: Personal Sacrifices	28
16	Chapter 16: The Future of Cross-Continental Ventures	30
17	Chapter 17: Inspiring the Next Generation	32

1

Chapter 1: The Global Visionaries

In the ever-shifting landscape of global business, certain individuals have transcended borders to create empires that span continents. These visionaries harness their unique perspectives to bridge countries and cultures, bringing innovation and progress wherever they go. The first chapter explores the rise of these trailblazers and their initial forays into cross-continental ventures.

Imagine a world where borders blur and the spirit of collaboration transcends geographical constraints. This is the realm of the global visionaries, the billionaires who possess the rare ability to see beyond national boundaries and unite disparate markets. From the bustling streets of New York to the vibrant markets of Lagos, these trailblazers have harnessed the power of global connectivity to build empires that span continents.

Their stories often begin with a spark of inspiration, a vision that compels them to break free from conventional norms and venture into uncharted territories. Driven by an insatiable curiosity and a deep desire to make a difference, these visionaries embark on journeys that take them far from their home shores. They recognize the immense potential of cross-continental ventures, not just for personal gain, but for the greater good of humanity.

One such visionary is Maria Rodriguez, a tech mogul who grew up in a small town in Spain. With a keen interest in technology and a passion for solving real-world problems, Maria founded her first startup in her garage.

Her innovative solutions quickly gained traction, attracting the attention of investors from around the world. Recognizing the potential for global impact, Maria expanded her operations to Silicon Valley, where she forged partnerships with industry giants and established a presence in the heart of the tech world.

Similarly, Adekunle Johnson, a Nigerian entrepreneur, saw an opportunity to bridge the gap between the African and European markets. Adekunle's journey began in Lagos, where he launched a successful e-commerce platform that catered to the unique needs of African consumers. Driven by a vision to connect Africa with the rest of the world, he established strategic alliances with European companies, paving the way for seamless trade and cultural exchange.

These global visionaries understand that success in cross-continental ventures requires more than just business acumen; it demands a deep appreciation for cultural diversity and an unwavering commitment to creating value for all stakeholders. Their ability to navigate complex international landscapes, build lasting relationships, and adapt to ever-changing market dynamics sets them apart as true pioneers of the global economy.

As we delve deeper into the lives of these remarkable individuals, we will uncover the key factors that have propelled them to success. From their early beginnings to their strategic partnerships and innovative approaches, we will explore the unique journeys of these global visionaries who continue to inspire and shape the future of cross-continental business.

2

Chapter 2: The Early Days

Every mogul has humble beginnings. This chapter delves into the early lives of these billionaires, tracing their roots from modest upbringings to their first entrepreneurial endeavors. We explore the formative experiences that shaped their global outlooks and instilled in them the drive to connect disparate markets.

Our journey begins in the bustling city of Lagos, where Adekunle Johnson grew up in a modest household. His parents, both educators, instilled in him the values of hard work and perseverance. From a young age, Adekunle was fascinated by the possibilities that technology could bring to his community. He spent countless hours in the local library, teaching himself coding and dreaming of a future where he could use his skills to create positive change.

Across the globe, in the quaint town of Salamanca, Spain, a young Maria Rodriguez was equally driven by a passion for innovation. Growing up in a family of artisans, Maria was surrounded by creativity and craftsmanship. Her father, a skilled carpenter, taught her the importance of precision and attention to detail, while her mother, a talented painter, inspired her to think outside the box. These early influences nurtured Maria's curiosity and fueled her determination to explore the world beyond her small town.

As they embarked on their respective journeys, both Adekunle and Maria faced numerous challenges. Adekunle's first entrepreneurial venture was a small tech startup aimed at providing affordable internet access to underserved communities in Lagos. Despite limited resources and a lack of formal training, he tirelessly worked to develop innovative solutions that would bridge the digital divide. His perseverance paid off when his startup gained recognition and attracted the attention of international investors.

Meanwhile, Maria's journey took her to Barcelona, where she pursued a degree in engineering. She quickly distinguished herself as a brilliant student, earning scholarships and accolades for her groundbreaking research. However, her path was not without obstacles. As a woman in a male-dominated field, Maria often faced skepticism and discrimination. Undeterred, she continued to push boundaries, determined to prove that innovation knows no gender.

Their early experiences taught Adekunle and Maria invaluable lessons about resilience, adaptability, and the importance of thinking globally. They understood that true success lay not in their individual achievements, but in their ability to connect and collaborate with others across cultures and continents. These formative years laid the foundation for their future endeavors, shaping them into the global visionaries they would become.

In the next chapter, we will explore how these early experiences influenced Adekunle and Maria's approach to strategic alliances, enabling them to navigate complex international landscapes and build successful cross-continental ventures.

3

Chapter 3: Strategic Alliances

Successful cross-continental ventures often hinge on strategic partnerships. This chapter examines the pivotal alliances that these billionaires forged, enabling them to navigate complex international landscapes. From joint ventures to mergers and acquisitions, we uncover the secrets behind their successful collaborations.

Maria Rodriguez and Adekunle Johnson quickly realized that their ambitions could not be achieved in isolation. They understood that building a global empire required forming strategic alliances with like-minded individuals and organizations. For Maria, this meant partnering with tech giants in Silicon Valley who shared her vision of using technology to solve real-world problems. She collaborated with industry leaders to develop cutting-edge solutions that could be scaled globally, ensuring that her innovations reached markets far beyond Spain.

Adekunle, on the other hand, focused on bridging the gap between African and European markets. He identified key players in the European e-commerce sector and forged alliances that facilitated seamless trade and cultural exchange. By working closely with European companies, Adekunle was able to introduce African products to new markets, while also bringing European goods to African consumers. These partnerships not only expanded his business but also fostered mutual understanding and collaboration between the two regions.

Both Maria and Adekunle recognized the importance of aligning their goals with those of their partners. They approached alliances with a mindset of reciprocity, ensuring that all parties involved benefited from the collaboration. This approach fostered trust and long-lasting relationships, which were crucial for navigating the complexities of international business.

As we delve deeper into their stories, we will uncover the specific strategies and tactics they employed to build and maintain these strategic alliances. We will also explore the challenges they faced and how they overcame them, demonstrating the resilience and adaptability that define true global visionaries.

4

Chapter 4: Cultural Diplomacy

Navigating cultural differences is a hallmark of cross-continental success. In this chapter, we explore how these moguls became adept cultural diplomats, building bridges between diverse populations. We delve into their strategies for understanding and respecting local customs, which paved the way for smooth operations in foreign territories.

Maria Rodriguez and Adekunle Johnson understood that successful global ventures required more than just business acumen; they needed to be cultural diplomats. Maria's journey took her to various countries, each with its own unique customs and traditions. She immersed herself in local cultures, learning the languages and understanding the nuances that defined each society. This cultural empathy allowed her to connect with people on a deeper level, building trust and fostering cooperation.

Adekunle, too, was a master of cultural diplomacy. He recognized the importance of respecting local customs and traditions, and he made it a priority to integrate these elements into his business operations. By doing so, he not only gained the trust of local communities but also ensured that his ventures were seen as respectful and inclusive. This approach opened doors to new opportunities and allowed him to navigate the complexities of international markets with ease.

Their ability to bridge cultural divides was not just a matter of understanding; it was a commitment to creating value for all stakeholders. Maria and Adekunle demonstrated that true success in cross-continental ventures required empathy, respect, and a genuine desire to learn from others. As we continue to explore their stories, we will uncover the specific practices and strategies they used to navigate cultural differences and build lasting relationships across borders.

5

Chapter 5: Market Domination

With a solid foundation of alliances and cultural awareness, these moguls set their sights on market domination. This chapter chronicles their ambitious expansion plans, detailing the innovative approaches they employed to capture new markets and outmaneuver competitors on a global scale.

Armed with strategic alliances and a deep understanding of diverse cultures, Maria Rodriguez and Adekunle Johnson were poised for market domination. Maria's tech innovations quickly gained traction, and she expanded her operations to new markets in Asia and the Americas. She leveraged her partnerships to establish a global presence, using cutting-edge technologies to streamline operations and enhance communication across continents. Her ability to adapt to changing market conditions and anticipate future trends allowed her to stay ahead of competitors and maintain a competitive edge.

Adekunle's e-commerce platform continued to grow, capturing new markets in Africa and Europe. He introduced innovative solutions that catered to the unique needs of each region, from localized payment systems to tailored marketing strategies. His ability to understand and respond to the preferences of different markets allowed him to outmaneuver competitors and establish a dominant position in the global e-commerce landscape.

As we delve deeper into their journeys, we will explore the specific tactics and strategies they used to achieve market domination. We will uncover the challenges they faced, the risks they took, and the innovative approaches that set them apart as true pioneers of the global economy.

6

Chapter 6: The Role of Technology

Technology has been a game-changer for global business. This chapter highlights how these billionaires leveraged cutting-edge technologies to streamline operations, enhance communication, and drive innovation across continents. We examine their investments in tech and the transformative impact on their enterprises.

Maria Rodriguez and Adekunle Johnson were quick to recognize the transformative power of technology in driving global business. Maria's background in engineering and tech gave her a unique advantage, allowing her to develop innovative solutions that addressed real-world problems. She invested heavily in research and development, partnering with leading tech companies to create products that could be scaled globally. Her use of cutting-edge technologies, from artificial intelligence to blockchain, revolutionized her operations and enabled her to stay ahead of the curve.

Adekunle, too, leveraged technology to expand his e-commerce platform and enhance the customer experience. He introduced advanced logistics systems, enabling seamless cross-border deliveries and reducing shipping times. His investments in mobile technology allowed him to reach a wider audience, particularly in regions where access to traditional banking was limited. By embracing technology, Adekunle was able to drive innovation and create value for his customers on a global scale.

7

Chapter 7: Philanthropy Without Borders

Beyond business, many cross-continental moguls are also noted philanthropists. This chapter explores their charitable efforts, which often span multiple countries and cultures. We highlight their contributions to education, healthcare, and social initiatives, demonstrating their commitment to global betterment.

Maria Rodriguez and Adekunle Johnson understood that with great wealth came great responsibility. Both were committed to using their resources to make a positive impact on the world. Maria's philanthropic efforts focused on education and technology access. She established foundations that provided scholarships to underprivileged students and funded tech labs in underserved communities. Her initiatives aimed to bridge the digital divide, ensuring that young minds around the world had the tools they needed to succeed in the digital age.

Adekunle's philanthropy was equally impactful, with a focus on healthcare and economic development in Africa. He funded clinics and hospitals in rural areas, providing much-needed medical services to underserved populations. His investments in microfinance programs helped small businesses thrive, creating jobs and lifting communities out of poverty. By addressing critical issues such as health and economic empowerment, Adekunle's philanthropic efforts had a far-reaching impact on the lives of many.

Both Maria and Adekunle's philanthropic endeavors demonstrated their

CHAPTER 7: PHILANTHROPY WITHOUT BORDERS

commitment to creating a better world. They understood that true success was not measured solely by financial gain, but by the positive change they could bring to society. Their efforts inspired others to follow suit, fostering a culture of giving and social responsibility among the global business community.

8

Chapter 8: Crisis Management

Global ventures are not without challenges. This chapter delves into the crises these billionaires faced, from economic downturns to geopolitical tensions. We explore their crisis management strategies, showcasing their resilience and ability to adapt in the face of adversity.

Maria Rodriguez and Adekunle Johnson encountered their fair share of crises throughout their careers. From economic recessions to geopolitical tensions, they faced numerous challenges that tested their resilience and adaptability. Maria's tech company was hit hard by the global financial crisis, forcing her to make tough decisions to keep her business afloat. She implemented cost-cutting measures, restructured her operations, and sought new revenue streams to weather the storm. Her ability to pivot and adapt to changing market conditions was key to her company's survival and eventual recovery.

Adekunle, too, faced significant challenges, particularly in navigating the complex political landscape of Africa. His e-commerce platform was threatened by regulatory changes and political instability in some of the markets he operated in. To address these challenges, Adekunle employed a proactive approach, engaging with policymakers and building strong relationships with local governments. His ability to anticipate and mitigate risks allowed him to navigate these crises and emerge stronger.

CHAPTER 8: CRISIS MANAGEMENT

Their experiences in crisis management highlighted the importance of resilience, adaptability, and strategic thinking. By staying calm under pressure and making informed decisions, Maria and Adekunle were able to overcome obstacles and continue their global ventures. Their stories serve as valuable lessons for aspiring entrepreneurs on the importance of crisis management in building and sustaining successful businesses.

9

Chapter 9: Leadership Styles

Leadership is key to managing cross-continental enterprises. In this chapter, we examine the diverse leadership styles of these moguls, from autocratic to collaborative approaches. We analyze how their leadership has evolved over time and the impact on their global operations.

Maria Rodriguez and Adekunle Johnson exhibited distinct leadership styles that were instrumental in their success. Maria's leadership was characterized by a collaborative approach, emphasizing teamwork and open communication. She believed in empowering her employees and fostering a culture of innovation and creativity. Her inclusive leadership style encouraged diverse perspectives and ideas, driving her company's growth and success.

Adekunle's leadership, on the other hand, was more strategic and visionary. He was known for his ability to see the big picture and make bold decisions that positioned his company for long-term success. While he valued input from his team, Adekunle was not afraid to take decisive action when necessary. His visionary leadership style inspired confidence and motivated his employees to strive for excellence.

Both leadership styles had their strengths and played a crucial role in their global ventures. Maria's collaborative approach fostered a sense of community and belonging, while Adekunle's strategic vision ensured that his company remained competitive in the global market. As we delve deeper into their leadership journeys, we will explore how their styles evolved over time and the impact they had on their global operations.

10

Chapter 10: The Power of Branding

Branding is crucial for global recognition. This chapter explores how these billionaires crafted and maintained powerful brands that resonate across cultures. We delve into their marketing strategies, brand positioning, and the importance of maintaining a consistent brand identity.

Maria Rodriguez and Adekunle Johnson understood the power of branding in establishing a global presence. Maria's tech company became synonymous with innovation and quality, thanks to her strategic branding efforts. She invested heavily in marketing and public relations, ensuring that her brand was recognized and respected worldwide. Her emphasis on maintaining a consistent brand identity across all markets helped build trust and loyalty among customers.

Adekunle's e-commerce platform also benefited from strong branding. He positioned his brand as a trusted and reliable provider of quality products, catering to the unique needs of African consumers. His marketing strategies emphasized the cultural richness and diversity of the African continent, resonating with both local and international audiences. By highlighting the uniqueness of his brand, Adekunle was able to differentiate his company from competitors and establish a strong market presence.

Both Maria and Adekunle's branding efforts were instrumental in their success. They understood that a strong brand could create a lasting impression and drive customer loyalty. Their stories highlight the importance of strategic branding and the impact it can have on global ventures.

11

Chapter 11: Mentorship and Legacy

Many of these moguls are not just focused on their own success but also on nurturing the next generation of leaders. This chapter highlights their mentorship efforts and the legacy they aim to leave behind. We explore how they are grooming future leaders to continue their cross-continental missions.

Maria Rodriguez and Adekunle Johnson understood the importance of mentorship in shaping the future of global business. Maria established mentorship programs within her tech company, providing young professionals with the guidance and support they needed to thrive in the industry. She personally mentored several rising stars, sharing her insights and experiences to help them navigate the complexities of the tech world. Her commitment to nurturing talent ensured that her legacy would continue through the next generation of innovators.

Adekunle, too, was passionate about mentorship. He founded an entrepreneurship academy in Lagos, where aspiring business leaders could learn from his experiences and gain the skills needed to succeed in the global market. Adekunle's mentorship efforts extended beyond formal programs; he often took the time to connect with young entrepreneurs, offering advice and encouragement. His dedication to fostering talent ensured that his vision of a connected and prosperous Africa would be carried forward by future leaders.

CHAPTER 11: MENTORSHIP AND LEGACY

Both Maria and Adekunle's mentorship efforts were driven by a desire to give back to their communities and create lasting change. They recognized that their success was not just about personal achievements but about the impact they could have on others. Their legacy is one of inspiration, empowerment, and a commitment to nurturing the next generation of global visionaries.

12

Chapter 12: Sustainable Ventures

Sustainability is becoming increasingly important in global business. This chapter examines how these billionaires are incorporating sustainable practices into their operations. We look at their efforts to reduce environmental impact and promote social responsibility on a global scale.

Maria Rodriguez and Adekunle Johnson were pioneers in integrating sustainability into their business models. Maria's tech company adopted eco-friendly practices, from energy-efficient data centers to sustainable product design. She also invested in renewable energy projects, ensuring that her operations minimized their environmental footprint. Maria's commitment to sustainability was not just about corporate social responsibility; it was a core part of her business strategy, driving innovation and attracting socially conscious customers.

Adekunle's e-commerce platform also embraced sustainability. He implemented green logistics practices, using electric vehicles for deliveries and reducing packaging waste. Adekunle's efforts extended to supporting sustainable development projects in Africa, from clean water initiatives to reforestation programs. His focus on sustainability not only benefited the environment but also created positive social and economic impacts for local communities.

Both Maria and Adekunle demonstrated that sustainability and profitability could go hand in hand. Their commitment to sustainable ventures set them apart as leaders in the global business community, inspiring others to follow suit and prioritize social and environmental responsibility.

13

Chapter 13: Navigating Regulatory Hurdles

Operating in multiple countries comes with regulatory challenges. This chapter delves into the regulatory hurdles these moguls faced and their strategies for compliance. We explore how they navigate complex legal landscapes to ensure their ventures thrive.

Maria Rodriguez and Adekunle Johnson encountered numerous regulatory challenges as they expanded their global ventures. Maria's tech company faced stringent data privacy regulations in various countries, requiring her to implement robust compliance measures. She established a dedicated legal team to navigate the complex regulatory landscape and ensure that her operations adhered to local laws. Maria's proactive approach to compliance allowed her to build trust with regulators and customers, ensuring the long-term success of her business.

Adekunle's e-commerce platform faced regulatory hurdles related to cross-border trade and consumer protection. He worked closely with legal experts to understand and comply with the regulations in each market he operated in. Adekunle's ability to navigate these challenges was instrumental in building a trusted and reliable platform for his customers. His compliance efforts also included advocacy for fair and transparent regulations, working with policymakers to create a more conducive environment for international trade.

CHAPTER 13: NAVIGATING REGULATORY HURDLES

Their experiences highlight the importance of understanding and adhering to regulatory requirements in global business. By prioritizing compliance and building strong relationships with regulators, Maria and Adekunle were able to navigate the complexities of international markets and ensure the sustainability of their ventures.

14

Chapter 14: Innovation and Adaptation

Innovation is the lifeblood of global business. This chapter highlights the innovative solutions these billionaires implemented to stay ahead of the curve. We examine their willingness to adapt to changing market conditions and their role as pioneers in their respective industries.

Maria Rodriguez and Adekunle Johnson were relentless innovators, constantly seeking new ways to enhance their businesses and create value for their customers. Maria's tech company was known for its groundbreaking products, from smart devices to advanced software solutions. She fostered a culture of innovation within her organization, encouraging employees to experiment and take risks. Maria's willingness to embrace new ideas and technologies allowed her company to stay ahead of the competition and maintain its position as a market leader.

Adekunle's e-commerce platform was also a hub of innovation. He introduced features that revolutionized the online shopping experience, from personalized recommendations to seamless payment solutions. Adekunle's ability to adapt to changing market conditions and anticipate future trends was key to his success. He invested in research and development, constantly exploring new ways to enhance his platform and meet the evolving needs of his customers.

Their commitment to innovation and adaptation set Maria and Adekunle apart as pioneers in their respective industries. They understood that staying

CHAPTER 14: INNOVATION AND ADAPTATION

ahead of the curve required a willingness to embrace change and take risks. Their stories serve as valuable lessons for aspiring entrepreneurs on the importance of innovation and adaptability in building successful global ventures.

15

Chapter 15: Personal Sacrifices

Building cross-continental empires often requires personal sacrifices. This chapter explores the personal challenges these moguls faced, from family pressures to health issues. We delve into how they balanced their personal lives with the demands of their global enterprises.

Maria Rodriguez and Adekunle Johnson experienced significant personal sacrifices on their journeys to success. For Maria, the relentless pursuit of innovation and expansion meant long hours and constant travel. The demands of her tech empire often left little time for personal relationships and leisure. Maria faced periods of burnout and isolation, but she remained steadfast in her commitment to her vision. She found solace in the support of her close-knit team, who shared her passion and dedication.

Adekunle's journey was similarly marked by personal sacrifices. As he expanded his e-commerce platform across continents, he faced immense pressure to deliver results. The demands of managing a global enterprise took a toll on his health, leading to stress and exhaustion. Adekunle struggled to find a balance between his work and personal life, often missing important family events and milestones. Despite these challenges, he remained driven by his vision of connecting African markets with the world.

Both Maria and Adekunle's experiences highlight the personal costs of building cross-continental empires. Their stories serve as a reminder that success often comes at a price, and the importance of finding a balance

CHAPTER 15: PERSONAL SACRIFICES

between professional and personal life. By acknowledging and addressing these challenges, they were able to persevere and continue their global missions.

16

Chapter 16: The Future of Cross-Continental Ventures

As the world becomes more interconnected, the future of cross-continental ventures looks promising. This chapter speculates on the future trends and opportunities in global business. We explore how these moguls are positioning themselves to capitalize on emerging markets and technologies.

Maria Rodriguez and Adekunle Johnson are optimistic about the future of cross-continental ventures. They recognize that the world is becoming increasingly interconnected, creating new opportunities for global business. Maria is particularly excited about the potential of emerging technologies, such as artificial intelligence and blockchain, to revolutionize industries and drive innovation. She continues to invest in research and development, positioning her company to capitalize on these advancements and stay ahead of the curve.

Adekunle sees tremendous potential in the growing African market. He believes that Africa's youthful population and rapid urbanization will drive economic growth and create new opportunities for cross-continental ventures. Adekunle is focused on expanding his e-commerce platform to reach more consumers across the continent, while also exploring opportunities in other sectors, such as fintech and renewable energy.

CHAPTER 16: THE FUTURE OF CROSS-CONTINENTAL VENTURES

Both Maria and Adekunle are committed to staying at the forefront of global business, continuously adapting to changing market conditions and embracing new technologies. Their forward-thinking approach ensures that they remain leaders in their respective industries, inspiring the next generation of entrepreneurs to pursue cross-continental ventures.

17

Chapter 17: Inspiring the Next Generation

The final chapter aims to inspire the next generation of entrepreneurs. We reflect on the lessons learned from these cross-continental moguls and provide actionable insights for aspiring global business leaders. We emphasize the importance of vision, perseverance, and cultural empathy in building successful cross-continental ventures.

Maria Rodriguez and Adekunle Johnson's journeys are filled with valuable lessons for aspiring entrepreneurs. Their stories demonstrate the importance of having a clear vision and the perseverance to pursue it, even in the face of challenges. They show that success is not just about individual achievements but about creating value for others and making a positive impact on the world.

One key takeaway from their experiences is the importance of cultural empathy in building cross-continental ventures. Maria and Adekunle's ability to understand and respect diverse cultures allowed them to navigate complex international landscapes and build lasting relationships. Their commitment to cultural diplomacy and inclusivity was instrumental in their success.

Aspiring entrepreneurs can also learn from Maria and Adekunle's willingness to embrace change and innovation. Their stories highlight the importance of staying ahead of the curve and continuously seeking new opportunities for growth. By fostering a culture of innovation and adaptability, entrepreneurs can ensure the long-term success of their global ventures.

Ultimately, Maria and Adekunle's legacies are not just about their business achievements but about the inspiration and empowerment they provide to others. Their journeys serve as a testament to the power of vision, perseverance, and cultural empathy in building successful cross-continental ventures. As we conclude this book, we hope that their stories will inspire the next generation of global visionaries to pursue their dreams and create a better world.

The Cross-Continental Moguls: Billionaires Who Bridge Countries and Cultures

In a world where borders often divide, some visionaries have found ways to connect and unify. "The Cross-Continental Moguls: Billionaires Who Bridge Countries and Cultures" takes readers on an inspiring journey through the lives of extraordinary billionaires who have transcended geographical constraints to build empires that span continents.

From their humble beginnings to their rise as global powerhouses, this book delves into the personal and professional journeys of these remarkable individuals. Each chapter highlights their innovative approaches, strategic alliances, and the unique challenges they faced in navigating diverse cultural landscapes.

Readers will explore how these moguls leveraged cutting-edge technologies, built lasting relationships, and embraced cultural diplomacy to create thriving cross-continental ventures. The book also sheds light on their philanthropic efforts, sustainable practices, and the legacy they aim to leave behind, inspiring the next generation of global leaders.

"The Cross-Continental Moguls" is a testament to the power of vision, perseverance, and cultural empathy. It celebrates the achievements of those who dare to think beyond borders, demonstrating that true success is measured not just by financial gain, but by the positive impact one can make on the world.

www.ingramcontent.com/pod-product-compliance
Lightning Source LLC
LaVergne TN
LVHW020501080526
838202LV00057B/6083